Donated to Ogden LRC

Happy Reading!

The PTC

TWENTY-ODD DUCKS

DUCKS

WHY, EVERY PUNCTUATION MARK COUNTS!

by
LYNNE TRUSS

illustrated by
BONNIE TIMMONS

G. P. PUTNAM'S SONS

INTRODUCTION

Do you have a favorite punctuation mark? I think mine is the hyphen. Lots of punctuation marks are for keeping words apart, but the hyphen does a lovely thing: it gets two words to hold hands, neatly, so that we can see they are related. You see, without the hyphen, twenty-odd ducks might not mean "around twenty ducks." It might mean all the ducks are odd! Without the hyphen, a blue-whale expert stops being "a person who knows all about blue whales" and becomes a person who is probably blue himself!

This book is all about how punctuation does two important things in writing: first, it keeps words in groups so the intended meaning will come through to the reader. It herds them into the right corrals, if you like, so there's less chance of their getting mixed up. On top of that, though, some punctuation marks add the tone of voice so that the reader knows whether you're asking a question, or making a statement, or shouting. By the end of the book, I'm sure you will be convinced of one thing: every punctuation mark counts.

Happy punctuating,

Lynne Truss

"Where do you think we're taking you? To the dungeon?"

"Where do you think? We're taking you to the dungeon."

These are Jack's parents; who could be happier?

These are Jack's parents, who could be happier.

William brought an extra large pizza.

William brought an extra-large pizza.

"Do you know who came last night? Santa Claus," said my mom.

"Do you know who came last night?" Santa Claus said. "My mom."

The king walked and talked.
Half an hour after, his head was cut off.

The king walked and talked
half an hour after his head was cut off.

"The punctuation test is today."

"The punctuatio

"The punctuation test is today?"

"The punctuation test is today!"

Our ancient-history teacher went to Egypt.

Our ancient history teacher went to Egypt.

The cowboy roped the steer (on his horse).

The cowboy roped the steer on his horse.

"This is Sharky, who lost a tooth."

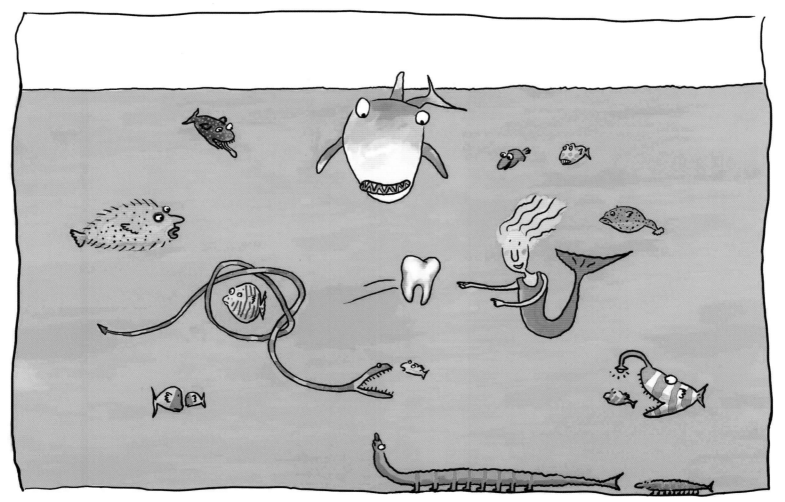

"This is Sharky. Who lost a tooth?"

The queen: without her, dinner is noisy.

The queen, without her dinner, is noisy.

"How many shoes do you need!"

"How many shoes do you need?"

The pirates (with red beards) shared the treasure.

The pirates with red beards shared the treasure!

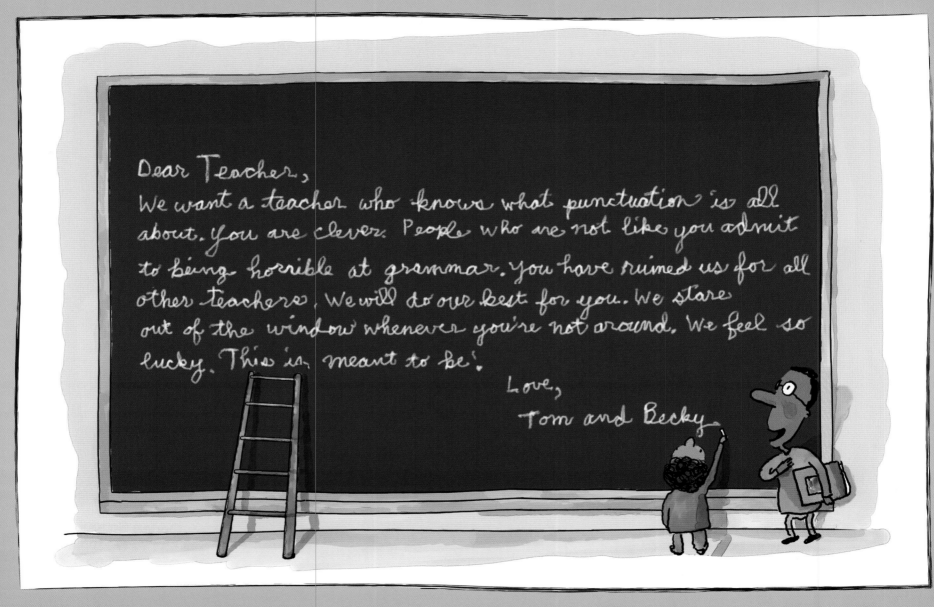

WHY, EVERY PUNCTUATION MARK COUNTS!

**"Where do you think we're taking you?
To the dungeon?"**
With question marks after *you* and *dungeon*,
both sentences are questions.

**"Where do you think? We're
taking you to the dungeon."**
The question mark after *think* makes the first sentence
a question, and the period after *dungeon* makes the
second sentence a statement.

These are Jack's parents; who could be happier?
The semicolon makes *These are Jack's parents* and *who
could be happier* two separate clauses. The question mark
after *happier* makes this a rhetorical question.

These are Jack's parents, who could be happier.
With a comma, *who could be happier* modifies *Jack's parents*.

**William brought an
extra large pizza.**
Without a hyphen, *extra* and *large* modify *pizza* separately.

**William brought an
extra-large pizza.**
With a hyphen, *extra* modifies *large*.

**"Do you know who came last night?
Santa Claus," said my mom.**
With the comma and quotation mark after *Claus*,
the mom is speaking.

**"Do you know who came last night?"
Santa Claus said. "My mom."**
With the quotation mark after *night*, the period after *said*, and quotation
marks surrounding *My mom*, Santa Claus is speaking.

**The king walked and talked.
Half an hour after, his head was cut off.**
With the period after *talked*, the actions of that sentence are
complete. The comma separates the prepositional phrase
Half an hour after from the clause *his head was cut off.*

**The king walked and talked half an hour
after his head was cut off.**
Without a period and comma,
the order of the actions is different.

**"The punctuation
test is today."**
The period makes this
a statement.

**"The punctuation
test is today?"**
The question mark
makes this a question.

**"The punctuation
test is today!"**
The exclamation point makes
this an exclamation.

Our ancient-history teacher went to Egypt.
With a hyphen, *ancient* modifies *history*.

Our ancient history teacher went to Egypt.
Without a hyphen, *ancient* and *history* modify *teacher*.

The cowboy roped the steer (on his horse).
In parentheses, *on his horse* modifies *cowboy*.

The cowboy roped the steer on his horse.
Without parentheses, *on his horse* modifies *steer*.

"This is Sharky, who lost a tooth."
With the comma after *Sharky*, *who lost a tooth* refers to Sharky.

"This is Sharky. Who lost a tooth?"
The period after *Sharky* ends a sentence. With a question mark after *tooth*, the speaker is asking a question.

The queen: without her, dinner is noisy.
The colon indicates that the text following it describes the queen. The comma separates the prepositional phrase *without her* from the clause *dinner is noisy*.

The queen, without her dinner, is noisy.
The commas on either side of *without her dinner* set off information that is not essential to the meaning of the sentence.

"How many shoes do you need!"
The exclamation point makes this an exclamation.

"How many shoes do you need?"
The question mark makes this a question.

The pirates (with red beards) shared the treasure.
The parentheses enclose information that is not essential to the sentence.

The pirates with red beards shared the treasure.
Without parentheses, *with red beards* applies to only certain pirates.

To Gemma.

—L. T.

Thank you to Kelley Wigren, Kristen Conrad and Elizabeth Deininger of Angier Elementary School, Newton, Massachusetts, and the teachers of Santa Cruz Catholic School, Tucson, Arizona, for help with the punctuation explanations.

G. P. PUTNAM'S SONS. A division of Penguin Young Readers Group. Published by The Penguin Group. Penguin Group (USA) Inc., 375 Hudson Street, New York, NY 10014, U.S.A. Penguin Group (Canada), 90 Eglinton Avenue East, Suite 700, Toronto, Ontario M4P 2Y3, Canada (a division of Pearson Penguin Canada Inc.). Penguin Books Ltd, 80 Strand, London WC2R 0RL, England. Penguin Ireland, 25 St. Stephen's Green, Dublin 2, Ireland (a division of Penguin Books Ltd.). Penguin Group (Australia), 250 Camberwell Road, Camberwell, Victoria 3124, Australia (a division of Pearson Australia Group Pty Ltd). Penguin Books India Pvt Ltd, 11 Community Centre, Panchsheel Park, New Delhi - 110 017, India. Penguin Group (NZ), 67 Apollo Drive, Rosedale, North Shore 0632, New Zealand (a division of Pearson New Zealand Ltd). Penguin Books (South Africa) (Pty) Ltd, 24 Sturdee Avenue, Rosebank, Johannesburg 2196, South Africa. Penguin Books Ltd, Registered Offices: 80 Strand, London WC2R 0RL, England.

Published simultaneously in Canada. Manufactured in China by South China Printing Co. Ltd. Text set in Handwriter bold. Library of Congress Cataloging-in-Publication Data Truss, Lynne. Twenty-odd ducks: Why, every punctuation mark counts! / Lynne Truss; illustrated by Bonnie Timmons. p. cm. 1. English language–Punctuation–Juvenile literature. I. Timmons, Bonnie. II. Title. PE1450.T757 2008 428.2–dc22 2007045386 ISBN 978-0-399-25058-3

1 3 5 7 9 10 8 6 4 2